A User's Guide for Fifty S
Hot Tips for Couples to S
(Plus, a one-page cheat sheet)

By Jennifer Slingerland Ryan, M.Ed., LPC
Psychotherapist

To my husband for his willingness to live out the steps in this user's guide on a daily basis.

Table of Contents

Why a User's Guide

No doubt you've heard the chatter in the news touting the latest "Mommy Porn," and perhaps you too have caught the "50 Shades Buzz." You may have downloaded it on your e-reader to find out what the hype is all about, or you may have opted not to read it after hearing the vast spectrum of reviews, deciding that erotica just isn't your thing. "It" is the hottest new book to hit the shelves: Fifty Shades of Grey. Regardless of what you've heard up to now, I invite you to experience this book from a different angle: as a relationship user's guide. I promise, you will not be disappointed!

Fifty Shades of Grey has taken the world by storm! Book sales quickly surpassed the 10 million mark. People everywhere have been scurrying to their local bookstore to pick up their copies. That is, if they can't download on their e-reader, which is the preferable method, because at the end of Fifty Shades of Grey, readers will immediately want to download and read Fifty Shades Darker, and of course, Fifty Shades Freed. Never mind the fact that it is a bit embarrassing for some to actually hold this steamy read in their hands while in public, and heaven forbid we women read something erotic! This would most certainly mean the reader was enjoying their little fictional getaway, and we couldn't have that!

The Fifty Shades Trilogy is a tale of two people falling in love; facing, then finding peace with the demons in their lives; experiencing unconditional love; and healing. Oh, and it's also got some really hot sex. Consequently, it is the sex that has some quite fearful of cracking open the pages of this little gem. I deliberately use the word "fearful" because if you've read the negative reviews of this story, no doubt you've seen but a small glimpse of the components of this trilogy including BDSM (bondage, dominance, sadism, and masochism) and erotica. Make no mistake, most people love this book for the hot lovemaking, sure, but if you read this entire series and aren't drawn to the love story that ensues between these two characters, you may have sadly missed out on some foundational principles we can all use in our own relationships.

To clarify, yes, I am suggesting we use Fifty Shades of Grey as a guidebook of sorts, in our own relationships. This fictional work of art has a bounty of lessons we can all sink our teeth into (pun intended)! From spicing things up sexually to finding peace and contentment in an otherwise dull relationship, if you can make yourself get past the BDSM overtones and explicit sex scenes you may not be accustomed to reading, you'll find some great tips to stimulate emotional connection in your relationship. And yes, even your sex life will be rejuvenated if you follow these simple tips I'll be providing for you.

Hello, my name is Jennifer Slingerland Ryan, and I am addicted to Fifty Shades of Grey. I'm also a marriage and family therapist. I've worked with couples and adult individuals for over 10 years using some of the best couple's therapy material available, including John Gottman's "Seven Principles for Making Marriage Work," Gary Chapman's "Five Love Languages," and David Burn's "Feeling Good Together." These are my favorites and most suggested books for the couples I treat. Now I have a new recommendation for some: Fifty Shades of Grey and this nifty little user's guide you're now reading. Many of my clients - women, men, and couples equally – seek counsel individually and with their partners disgruntled in their relationship, and in their sex lives. This series has spiced up their sexual and emotional connectedness in and out of the bedroom.

Admittedly, the reviews for this popular read, despite the buzz, didn't immediately have me racing to pick up a copy. I'm not one to indulge in the latest fad series just because everyone else is doing it. When a good friend texted and implored me to read the book, claiming she was slightly obsessed and needed someone to talk to about it, however, I went ahead and gave in - for her, of course. That's what friends do. We read soft-core porn for each other.

That's my story, and I'm sticking to it!

Let me be completely upfront and honest by saying I was utterly taken with the books immediately. I read the first book, Fifty Shades of Grey in less than 24 hours, abandoning my kids in its wake, and hanging on its every word. Then, at approximately 12:32am, when I finally reached the end of book one, I quickly downloaded book two, Fifty Shades Darker, and stayed up hours into the early morning reading. Fifty Shades Darker was read within the next 24 hours. Then, following suit, I downloaded Fifty Shades Freed, and read this last piece more slowly, willing it not to end. I had become smitten with Christian Grey and this love story, and I took my sweet time getting through the final words by E.L. James, not wanting the fairytale to end. When it did end, I opened up book one and began again.

I felt a little crazy, absolutely. But what helped me feel more normal was hearing from friend after friend, how they also were taken with this love story. We all wanted to talk about it, and we all had the same things to say.

I had to finally admit to my husband what had my devoted and undivided attention. I confided that I was having a love affair with a fictional story and Christian Grey, the lead character in the Fifty Shades Trilogy, and that I secretly wanted to be whipped and handcuffed and have sex at the drop of a penny. I dreamt of sexy, passionate foreplay with my husband that lasted all day - the kind he would have engaged in since my eyes opened that morning and continued well into the evening. I began to long with sexual desire, hoping for his texts professing his love and arousal saying, "I can't wait to get you home..." Except... those texts didn't come, and I wasn't sure I really wanted to be bound and gagged anyway. Maybe just spanked. And only if he engaged in foreplay all day long. Okay, I digress...

Here's the thing: All the women I confided in - they also confiding in me - felt the same way. We all felt a little silly, yet we were aware there was something missing in our relationships that we needed to address. When my husband read one review to me about the book he said the lead character, Ana, was lacking self-respect. My husband was confused. Why would I want to be degraded, hit, spanked, and left to feel worthless, with no self-respect?

Then there were the articles and reviews that said this exact thing over and over again - this book series portrays a woman lacking worth, and the series is overall oppressive to women. It takes their voice away, they claimed, and it encourages violence. If this is so, why can't women get enough? Why is this "Mommy Porn" so hot? Why are we so smitten with Christian Grey?

I have answers! I'll be the voice of insight in this handy little relationship guide you're now reading, letting you know precisely what women are talking about, and what to do about it. Hopefully there will be no shades of gray, only concrete, black and white answers. Are men reading and talking about this series? I can't answer that with confidence. I can only give my experience and my professional insight.

This book series is genius. Honestly, genius. As a marriage and family therapist, I would love to assign this book as homework for many of my clients, except I worry that the REAL message wouldn't be conveyed. The real message isn't one of abuse, beatings, sodomy, masochism, or oppression. The real message is one of trust and love, which I'll cover in depth in part 7 of this guide.

Kudos to E.L. James for an incredible series. One that is not just about hot sex, but make no mistake, James invigorates the senses! Her sexual descriptions are extraordinary, and women all around the country are itching for more passion, intimacy, foreplay, and emotional connection. This story is robust, thoroughly developing the main characters and their accelerated love affair. Ms. James clearly has a knack for understanding the core of what makes a relationship a hot one (and it's not JUST the floggers and spreader bars!).

I am frankly surprised by the reviews, claiming this book is nothing more than "Mommy Porn." It seems as if the reviewers read about half of the first book, formed an opinion, and wrote diminished, uninformed critiques. For those of us who have read this trilogy, those reviews are transparent - it is easy to see the reviewers haven't read the full trilogy. As a relationship counselor, I think those reviewers have completely missed the mark. How could you not read this book, no matter who you are, and feel not only turned on, but aching to hear more? How could you not be left wondering why Christian Grey has chosen this life for himself, and how Ana Steele is going to get out of this mess she's in, especially when they can't seem to keep their hands off each other?

Let me stop right here and give fair warning. I am going to talk about all three books, answering a few fundamental questions about sex, love, romance, and relationships. In doing so, I'm going to assume you, the reader, have gone through all three Shades of Grey books. I will also assume you are ready for an open discussion. Maybe you aren't going to read them, and only want to cut to the chase by reading this user's guide. That is fine, but you have been warned. I WILL reveal the full story, including the ending. If you have not read the books, you'll want to go read them now so I don't spoil anything for you.

Why does this series work? Why is it so hot? Why are women itching to have a little Christian Grey in their life? Why are people appalled that moms may actually ENJOY porn? And, most importantly, what can we learn from this book? In the end, that's what we want anyway, don't we? We want to be wowed by our partner. We want to know he is completely taken with our very presence. We want him to seduce us, make us writhe under his touch, then get out there and load the dishwasher with a smile on his face. I will seek to answer all of these questions throughout this guide. You'll want to keep up through the sex recommendations because part 7, the very last section of this guide, includes the most important recommendations for any relationship by far.

Okay, that may be a lot to ask. But here's the thing: Women WANT to have sex (almost) as much as their men do. Actually, it depends on the women and the men... we all want varying amounts. Let's make one thing clear though: we are sexual beings. All of us have sexual desires and want sex, and we want the sex to be hot. So, if couples are going to have some hot sex, it's high time we talk about how that's going to happen. The Shades of Grey trilogy gives many clues to what women want, and I'm going to lay them all out here.

Couples, consider this your sex and relationship user's guide. This trilogy has enraptured one or both of you because you want more in your relationship. If you can't quite put your finger on what the "more" is, you'll get more insight reading the Shades of Grey books and in this handy little relationship user's guide. My relationship guide is what women are talking about with their friends, and the sex and intimacy read in these pages can be mimicked, at least in part, in your own relationship. You can thank me later. :-)

Let's start from the top.

What immediately draws women to this book is the confidence in the main character, Christian Grey. He is elusive, but bold. He controls the room, is assertive, and is not shy about what he wants (or so it seems in the beginning). Okay yes, he is also a billionaire. But make no mistake, women aren't taken with this. It's not the money; it's the command he takes of his surroundings. Women are taken by his ability to be in control of himself and of a room. He is charming, charismatic, and a natural leader. He exudes confidence. We love this about Christian.

You want tangibles, I'm sure. Let's talk specifics about the confidence and boldness of Christian Grey and what this means for your own relationship.

1. Discuss the Unspoken Rules

Christian and Ana meet by chance encounter. Christian pursues Ana – he invites her to coffee then on a date one evening. In their next date, with the sexual tension rising, Christian puts the breaks on and proceeds to present Ana with a proposal. His proposition is of a different type of courtship. In fact, it's not really a courtship at all. Christian wants Ana to enter into a BDSM relationship with him. He presents her with a Non-Disclosure Agreement (NDA) and a set of rules. (I can only guess all high profile billionaires need an NDA? Maybe it is just the ones who are into beating their partners with floggers and canes.)

Christian tells Ana the rules are designed for safety and for pleasure, and so that they both have fulfilling sexual encounters. Ana is taken aback because she has never been presented with "rules" in a relationship before. They are audacious and strange. In fact, the rules are unlike anything she has experienced in her past courtships.

As a reader you think, "What?? Rules? I don't need RULES in my relationship." This is the first we hear of Christian's dominant/submissive world, and it's starting to feel quite bizarre, but...curious. True, no one wants to be controlled, of course. Few people want to relinquish power of their life, no matter how smitten and trusting you are with them. Some reviewers have even said Christian's rules are manipulative because they seek to get Ana to live a life of which she isn't accustomed. Let's take a closer look though…

<u>Sleep</u>: Christian Grey wants his partner to get at least seven hours of sleep a night. Uhm, hello? Motherhood? What Mom wouldn't want to have a guaranteed seven hours of sleep each night, our partner doing all he could to make that happen? Okay, sure, Christian wants her to be rested up so he can man-handle her sexually, but here's the thing…if you want sex with your partner, and when it's convenient for both of you, you're going to both need to be rested. Few will consent to anything more than quickie sex when they are tired.

When you want to have sex with your wife and she's been spit on, puked on, pooped on, and climbed on all day long, with demands thrown at her from all direction from the kids, AND she's running on only 4-5 hours of sleep, the last thing she wants to do is give you sex. It's not that she doesn't want sex, it's that she's freaking tired. And she stinks of kid. She doesn't feel at all sexy, and she doesn't want to give

One. More. Thing. To. One. More. Person. And that includes her body, to you. Unless, of course, she is rested, and you have provided her adequate assistance and relaxation to get her all prepped and ready for some adult play time!

Clothes: Mr. Grey wants Miss Steele (this is what they playfully begin to call each other) dressed in appropriate attire. In other words, he wants her sexy. He's even willing to provide the clothing for her. Now, I get that we aren't billionaires, and we don't have personal shoppers at Neiman Marcus. However, clothing matters. This brings to mind a time my husband looked at me squarely in the eyes and said, "Do you ever go out of the house (during the week)? Because I only see you in sweats and PJs." Good point well made as ever, Mr. Ryan. In fact, I completely slacked on pulling myself together – for him. During my work hours as a therapist, which happened to be during the same time as he was working, I would shower, shave, brush, tease, primp, pump, and put on my nice work clothes. By the time he made it home, I was already in my frumpy clothes again. He never got to see the "put together" wife he married. He only got to see the Mom who smelled like kid.

If we want to spice things up in the bedroom, we need to be cognizant of our hotness level. Our clothes, our hair, and having a conscious regard for body posture and energy, even with our spouse to whom we've been married for 15 years all matter.

Exercise: Christian wants his partner to exercise, and will provide her a trainer so she can do so at least four times per week. This seems a bit much, but who are we kidding? How hot is it to see a svelte, built, muscular man or woman? If we're being completely honest with ourselves, we will say that yes, we want to have a fit partner. Is that wrong or superficial? Not always. Attractiveness IS in the eye of the beholder, and most of the time the beholder likes to have someone who takes care of themselves physically. Exercise matters. For health and to look your best, a fit body is attractive to most.

Personal Habits / Hygiene: Mr. Grey would like Miss Steele to be primed, waxed and ready for sex at a moment's notice. For most, this is hard to do on a daily basis! How often have you decided you wouldn't shave today because it was cold outside, you would be wearing pants anyway, and no one would notice? Yeah, a lot. But how great does it feel to be waxed from head to toe? If you don't know how it feels to be waxed from head to toe, this might be a good time to find out. Waxing and shaving is a must. It's what we want for ourselves, it's what our men want from us, and it's what we want from our partner most of the time.

A friend recently told me she wasn't aware that most women groomed their under parts, including getting regularly waxed. She knows now because her husband requested she clean herself up! And now women, you know, too.

This topic falls right in line with having our men cleanly shaved (unless you specifically like stubble, and that's up for discussion), nails clean and trimmed, and all visible hair that should not be THERE – nose, ears, back – gone. We women don't want to see that, and we sure as heck don't want to watch you get RID of it. What I'm saying is this: Men and women both, keep yourself properly groomed. Wax, shave, shower, wash, spray, and spritz, and do it privately. Pull yourself together before you see your partner, preparing for your time together. Seeing your nasty toenails all over the bathroom floor, and your hair stubble lining your sink is a huge turn off.

Personal Safety: Christian wants no smoking, recreational drugs or drinking to excess. This goes without saying for most people (that is, unless you're both smokers, then you're all up in each other's smoky smell). Christian wants his woman to be safe. We want our partner to be safe, too! But more than just safety, being out of control with a substance is just…a real turnoff. And, the smell you emit after a hard night of drinking is just really disgusting. There's nothing charming about how you carry yourself or command the room around you when you've filled your brain with substances. This isn't just about personal safety; this is about being attractive and holding yourself together. If you want hot sex with your partner, keeping yourself composed and self-assured is so much more attractive than presenting yourself as slovenly and disheveled.

Personal Qualities: "Don't enter into sexual relations with anyone else, conduct yourself in a respectful manner, and realize your behavior is a direct reflection of your partner. Last, hold yourself accountable for any misdeeds, wrongdoings, and misbehavior." Yes, yes, yes, and YES. Most of us don't want our partners having sex outside the marriage, this should go without saying. (Certainly, this is a personal lifestyle choice between couples. Who am I to judge?) How you conduct yourself in public, realizing that your behavior is a direct reflection on your partner is huge! You are a team. And as a team, what you do together, and separate, matters. It's important that you realize how your behavior is impactful on anyone, including your partner and your relationship together. When you're strong and confident without your partner, that lets others know you're strong and confident together in your home. Few will deny the appeal of a respectful, self-assured partner. Strength and poise is a turn on.

Time and again I hear couples tell me how the beginnings of their relationships were really hot – great sex, their partner was very attentive, and there were no shards of cut toenail anywhere. But after a time, the relationship goes south. It's puzzling! Couples can't understand why they no longer have sex, aren't appealing to each other, and have fights all the time.

The rules may seem offensive, but examine them closely. When you get right down to it, you want these things for your partner, don't you? When you're attracted to a woman or man initially it's because they seem very well put together, right? The image we give off – the energy we bring to a room, the confidence we exude, and the cleanliness we have – all matter. Unspoken rules are in every relationship, and most marriages would do well to have rules such as these. If the rules are broken, it doesn't mean a spanking or a flogging. But at face value, can you argue with a clean, shaved, delicious partner, smiling and standing before you at the end of a long, hard work day? I didn't think so.

What to do now:

Tips for Men:

- If you're a dad and your wife stays at home with kids, help her get rest. You may think she sits around watching soap operas all day. Rest assured, she is not. You'll find she is more rested for your sexual advances the more you help.
- Make sure your clothes fit your body shape and are stain-free! Having a disheveled, unkempt man is a turnoff.
- Keep your beard trimmed and neat, nails trimmed, and all other hair appropriately shaved / waxed and neat.

Tips for Women:

- Wear clothes that fit your body type, but remember, while your man likes your curves, some things are best left to the imagination or covered altogether. Too much revealing is a turn off, especially when clothes are too tight and your…various body parts…begin to spill out. (I'm talking fat rolls here, ladies, not breasts.)

- Get a good bikini wax – regularly! And, keep your legs shaved, even in cold weather.

Tips for Couples:

- Have a discussion about unspoken rules in your relationship now. Talk about their importance, and decide together if there are some rules you'd like to change effective immediately.
- Get regular exercise. It tones your body and mind, keeping you physically fit and in a good mood. Walk together after dinner, jog together before work, go to the gym together, join a yoga class, or take an aerobics or kickboxing class.
- Don't smoke, drink or do drugs to excess – a real turn off!
- Notice how you represent yourself and your partner while in public. Remember, you're a team!

2. Ask "The Question" to Know What Turns Your Partner On

"Show me how you pleasure yourself," Christian said to Ana.

Uhm, excuse me?

Miss Steele is taken aback, but Mr. Grey persists and says, "Don't be coy, Ana. Show me how you make yourself come. I want to see."

Yes, that's right. Mr. Grey has requested that Miss Steele show him how she masturbates. She says no. Hell no! She will show him no such thing. How dare him!

But really? Why on earth would Christian even ask this question? What's it to him how she pleasures herself?

To set the scene: Christian and Ana have not had sex yet. They are negotiating the terms of their relationship (something few of us do, but having rules has merit, as we saw in the last section), and as they are about to have sex for the first time, Christian, wanting to please Ana, casually asks her to show him how she pleasures herself. She winces in horror, and denies his request (in fact, she denies having ever pleasured herself, which I don't believe happens often, but it is definitely possible). Ana didn't show him because she didn't know how to pleasure herself. On Christian's part, though, this is the perfect question.

Why?

Christian wants to know what Ana wants. The only way he is going to please her sexually is by touching her in a way that works for her. Not all women and men are created equally. Not all body parts are perfectly positioned. What turns you on may not turn another person on. The only way Christian is going to be able to satisfy Ana sexually is if he knows how she gives herself an orgasm, so he can mimic what she does. He wants to touch her where she touches herself. He can help her have an orgasm, if he knows how. He can help her find pleasure, if she shows him how she pleasures herself.

How many times have you EVER had this conversation with a partner? Probably none. And probably, when that discussion doesn't happen, there are some very disappointed adults in the marital bed.

The only way to know what your partner wants is to ask. Ask again, and ask again. And Do. As. She (or He!). Requests. When you get it wrong, ask again for a demo. Practice is the key to perfection, as we know. Don't pretend you know how to please your partner just because you've read a book or googled what you think you should know. The only way to know how to please your woman (or your man), is to be inquisitive. Ask him what he wants. Have her show you what it takes to pleasure herself. Don't be coy!

This rule goes for ALL sexual acts, not just plain old vanilla sex (i.e. missionary position). Your partner wants your touch with your fingers, your tongue, your penis, and any other mutually agreed upon object, but she definitely does not want you to touch her if you don't know what the heck you're doing with said object. It does nothing for your partner if you touch her with your fingers, but completely miss the mark. Likewise, your touch might be too fast, too slow, or just altogether wrong for what your partner needs. A touch that does nothing for her is a touch to turn you on, not her.

This discussion is for men and woman alike. How does your partner like their oral sex, if at all? Are you a skilled kisser? Do they like you to be vocal during sex; do they like you to wear sexy lingerie? Asking is very important.

If you want to turn your partner on, ask how you can touch in a way that is a turn on. Likewise, don't just assume that a tongue on your partner is going to automatically do the trick. It's what you do WITH your tongue, and where you place it, that matters. If you don't know what to do with your tongue, ask. It may be embarrassing, but not near as embarrassing as her faking an orgasm because she's completely bored or him dreading your advances because he's annoyed with what you think you know in the bedroom and with your partner's body.

He may claim he doesn't like to have his penis sucked, but perhaps it's that you do a bad job so he prefers you stick to just intercourse.

She'll be talking about the quality of your sexual pursuits with her girlfriends (maybe), and she won't want to repeat that scene again (definitely) if the scene is bad. Both of you will be avoiding sex at all costs, feigning exhaustion or sickness just to get out of it.

When your partner doesn't want to have sex, you'll be wondering what happened to their libido. Nothing is wrong with their libido, their libido is fine. What's wrong is that you may not know how to touch in a satisfying way, and you aren't interested in knowing because you’re too self-absorbed. Your partner doesn’t want to waste time with your inexperienced hands, mouth, or body.

What to do now:

Well into the marriage, it can be difficult to have a discussion about sexual preferences. But if your sex frequency is less than ideal, and you aren't enjoying yourself quite as much as you'd like, consider that one or both of you doesn't really enjoy how you're being touched. This topic comes up again and again in the privacy of my therapy office, but it’s not a topic you or your partner easily broaches, especially when you're the one who's dissatisfied. Openly discussing your sexual preferences - how and where you like to be touched - is the only way for you both to experience sexual satisfaction. Here are some probing questions to get you started:

- "We both want a better sex life. Will you show me how you like to be touched so I can please you?" (That's forward! And it's also a mega turn on.)
- "Watching you get aroused and have an orgasm makes me horny. How can I arouse you?" (SUPER forward, and major turn on once again!)
- "I want to explore your body, starting with your feet. Can I take off your shoes and give you a foot massage?" (Start with the feet, massage, kiss, lick, then move north, my friend! Explore your partner's body, and stay in tune to their body's response as you do.)

Tips for Men:

- Do you like to fellatio? Tell your partner how to do it so you like it.
- Do you like assisted masturbation? Teach your partner to do it how it most pleases you.

Tips for Women:

- Do you like cunnilingus? Teach your partner how to do it so you like it.
- Do you like to be touched and fingered? Tell your partner where and how strong to touch you.

Tips for Couples:

- Have a frank discussion about sex. Talk about oral sex, masturbation, hand jobs, tongue usage, and kissing. Say what you like and don't like.
- Be kind during your conversation and with your coaching! Finding out you've been doing it wrong is hard to hear, so use positives instead of negatives, such as, "I like when you do this…" or "It feels good when you ___."
- Don't be afraid to speak up when you need something different, but make sure your request is loving, nice and respectful.

Here's a tip: Anticipation is the key to seduction. While exploring each other, arousal will happen! But take it slow. Don't jump right into sex because you're both horny. Tease, kiss all over, touch her where she gets ignited, but don't rush things. Have your partner anticipate the end...it will make the orgasm even better! (And, she'll remember this next time, which means she'll want to have sex again soon.)

3. Discuss Your Sexual Fantasies

Mr. Grey, the Dominant, wants his partner, Miss Steele, to be his Submissive. The words alone make me shudder. They may make you shudder, too. But, let's look a bit closer at this proposal…

It doesn't take a rocket scientist to know that, in essence, Christian Grey wants total control over Anastasia Steele in the bedroom (well, in the playroom – the room he keeps all his toys, chains, whips and shackles in), and this doesn't feel good to most of us. Except…when it does.

Admit it. Most want our partners to take control at least some of the time, if not a majority of the time. You may not want her to beat you (or you might), but you want her to come on to you, tell you how sexy you are, rile you up, get you hot and bothered, and help you have your delicious orgasm. Women and men both anticipate the end result.

In a perfect world sex would come easily (no pun intended) – you'd both be having sex whenever you each wanted. You'll be MORE eager when you put some of these ideas into place.

Here's the thing: When you feel wanted, like your partner is just dying to have sex with you, and can't think of a single thing on the face of the planet except having mad sex with you RIGHT NOW, you'd do just about anything to make that happen. You'd also be willing to take a few risks and act out a few fantasies. Annnndd, some of these fantasies may involve cable ties or handcuffs. Just a plain, gray, necktie will also do. Or twine. Or a bathrobe tie for her wrists, her ankles or her thighs. Whatever you both prefer!

However, tying up and taking risks can happen only in certain circumstances, of course. It can only happen if it's consensual, and you agree you want to act out this fantasy. Indeed, there will be no tying up or even basic vanilla sex if your partner isn't turned on. You have to communicate your desire. Be seductive. Pine, yearn, and thirst after your partner; show your longing. I'm not talking about in the minutes just before sex, either. Seduction is happening now, even as you read this guide.

Tying your partner up doesn't mean you can disrespect boundaries. When your partner says no, they mean no. But they probably won't say no if you do it right – if you're both extremely turned on, you command control of the room, you exude self-confidence, you treat each other with the utmost respect and tenderness, and this is something you've both discussed and consented to previously. You can be warm with her wrists tied up. She expects you to be nothing but gentlemanly, tender and respectful. And then, give it to her - hard, soft, and all the ways in between.

So, Mr. Grey presented a contract for Miss Steele essentially outlining what they will and will not do sexually. They discuss, in no uncertain terms, what they both want while they're having sex. At first glance, you may be appalled. Not everyone wants to be hung from a carabiner on the ceiling while being screwed. (I suggest we not knock it until we try it, but that is just me.)

What's valuable about this contract?

What's valuable is that the couple is talking about their fantasies. And, it would behoove you to talk to your spouse about your fantasies, too. Acting on fantasies means they're no longer just fantasies - they are now reality.

Look, what happens in the kitchen is kitchen stuff. You cook, clean, make meals for the family and the kids. You're a domestic god or goddess. What happens in the family room during movie night is family fun – you pop some popcorn, pick a good flick you can all enjoy, and snuggle up together for some family fun. What you do in the bedroom is consensual, adult play. It is private, and it is up to you what you do in there. But you can't do anything except basic "let's-get-this-finished sex" if you don't talk about what else you can do beyond that.

You can be a bedroom god or goddess if you follow the rules I'm laying out for you here. Being a bedroom god, helping all your fantasies come true, will only happen if you talk about what your fantasies are. And then, deciding if it's safe, agreeable, and legal (yes, legal) to carry out some of your fantasies, have at it! (I throw the legal part in there because as a therapist, I've heard some pretty wild fantasies. Some of them were not legal and should not be acted on, ever. I'm not going to ruin the mood by talking about any of those here, but I suggest you be smart, or I'm with the majority of the population and will have no problem wishing you'd rot in jail for the duration of your life – without sex, I might add).

For the BDSM relationship Christian proposes, he suggests "limits." This is common of BDSM scenes, having both parties thoroughly discuss what they will and will not do sexually with each other. "Soft limits" refers to acts done only occasionally or during special circumstances. For example, one may only engage in cunnilingus if she takes a shower beforehand and thoroughly cleans herself. A "hard limit" explains what the person will not do under any circumstance, ever.

Discussing soft limits and hard limits with our partners just makes sense, doesn't it? But how many of us have this type of conversation since, never?

Christian opens a conversation with Ana to discuss their limits, including:

- Masturbation
- Cunnilingus
- Fellatio
- Swallowing Semen
- Vaginal Intercourse
- Vaginal Fisting
- Anal Intercourse
- Anal Fisting
- Vibrators
- Butt Plugs
- Dildos
- Other vaginal / anal toys

Some of those things make you cringe. Some of them make you curious. Some of them make you…excited. Which ones do you want to explore? Which ones does your partner want to explore? And how do you know? Because you're going to ask!

Furthermore, does your partner want to be bound with rope, leather cuffs, shackles, tape, or cable ties? Bound with nothing?

Does your partner want to be bound at the ankles, elbows, knees, ankles while kneeling, while standing, while lying down, or to the bedpost? Does she want to be blindfolded, spanked, or bit? Is she open to nipple clamps, hot wax or ice on her … parts? Or are most of these hard limits, no questions asked?

These are questions you thought you'd never ask. And maybe you don't want to ask them. Maybe this is too much for you and you aren't interested in the LEAST about any of these things because they're crazy and make you feel dirty and wrong. If so, that's fine. But I suggest you keep an open mind about what you want and what you don't want, and keep an open mind about what your PARTNER wants and does not want.

When two consenting adults decide to have their adult play time in the bedroom, in private, it's okay to kick things up a notch. It's okay to have fun. But the only way to explore those limits is to talk about them.

As I said, hard limits are the acts you absolutely will not tolerate, in no way, shape or form. It's okay to communicate this to your partner. If you've decided that you absolutely, 100%, will NOT swallow his semen, let him know. If you cannot envision yourself being tied up with twine in one million years, let him know that, too.

Communication really is what I'm getting at here. While most of our marital conversations don't contain questions about anal fisting and bondage, the conversations should involve questions seeking answers to how you envision having sex in the bedroom. It's okay to have those conversations! It's okay to explore yourself sexually. It's okay to have adult play time.

Do you need to write those down in a contract that you both sign? Well, of course not. Making yourself vulnerable while in discussion with your partner has its advantages. For starters, you find out what your partner wants sexually. You make fantasies a reality. Likewise, you have to be interested in what your spouse wants, and ask. When your partner says they want something, or do not want something, be respectful of it. When she says, "I want you to touch me this way and not that way," don't be offended. Be glad she told you. And then, try to perfect your method. You want her to do the same to you, don't you? You want to have fun in the bedroom, right? So, have the conversations, and have them more than once. Needs change, ideas change, and sometimes we become more bold and brave and ready to try new things. The sex conversation should happen regularly.

As I said, you don't have to have a written contract the way Christian wanted for Ana (and ultimately, they did not have, by the way, because they talked about what they wanted openly and honestly, and they trusted each other implicitly, so there was no need for writing those needs or wants in black and white), but you do have to have a conversation. Multiple conversations. That is, if you want to have a better relationship, and a better time in the bedroom.

Let's face it; we all want a better relationship in some way. And, better relationships ultimately have better sex. What I love about this book is not just that the sex is hot. In fact, the sex is really a sidebar. It's a symptom of something bigger and greater. The sex is on fire. There's magic between these two – they constantly want each other, beg for each other. They can't keep their minds off of each other when they're apart (or so it seems), and they can hardly keep their hands off of each other when they're together. They find ways to spice up their sex life constantly. Sex doesn't have to only happen in the bedroom, in one position, at the same time, all the time. That's just boring. When we get down to it, the real story of these books is about how Ana feels cherished and adored by Christian. He communicates his love for her, and what he wants to do to her sexually throughout the day. (I'll be talking more in depth about the relational aspects of Christian and Ana in part 7.)

In my conversations with friends who read this book, the same thing came up again and again. Sex, yes – we talked about the hot sex. But we talked about WHY the sex was hot. The sex was hot because the relationship was hot. The relationship – the communication they had with each other, the longing they had for each other, and the wanting they communicated in various ways – was hot. They knew how to keep the zest in the relationship!

What to do now:

Tips for Couples:

- Fifty Shades of Grey is a great conversation starter. Use the book to start a conversation about fantasies. If you've talked about fantasies in the past, take a leap out of your comfort zone and indulge your partner in part of the fantasy. If you haven't had a conversation about fantasies, but you have some, start small, offering up suggestions. For example, if your fantasy is to tie up your partner with restraints, hands behind his back start by grasping his hands above his head, immobilizing him. See how he responds, then broach the subject at another time about how much you liked it, and ask how much he liked it. Suggest using something else - a bathrobe tie or a necktie for example. Or, use your lacy panties. He might quite enjoy those tied on his wrists!

- If you're a man who wants your partner to swallow your semen after a blow job, bring it up during this discussion. If you are a woman who wants to try a vibrator, let your husband know, then schedule a trip to a sex shop together.

4. Engage in Minute-by-Minute Foreplay

Foreplay is happening right this minute. As you read this, your partner has preoccupied their thoughts with something like the kids, housework to be done, their job, running an errand or a good ole' erotic book. Whatever we focus on and have our minds on, is what leads us into action. So, doesn't it make sense to put YOU on your partner's mind? Don't you want her to pine for you? If so, put yourself in the middle of your partner's world.

Contrary to popular belief, foreplay doesn't only happen in the minutes before you have sex. Foreplay happens all day, every day. What you choose to do now will affect what happens in the bedroom - IF something happens. In the moments before sex, this is the time to enjoy each other and the arousal you've been creating throughout the day.

Christian was good at foreplay. He and Ana turned each other on throughout the day through emails, texts, body language, and verbal cues. When Ana hears the "ping" of her email, she anticipates a hot, sultry message from Christian communicating his desire to be with her. And, I'm not necessarily talking about sexting or getting graphic in email. I'm talking about just staying in touch, letting your partner know you are thinking of him, letting him know he's the most important thing on your agenda, and you can't wait to see him at the end of the day.

Domestic Duties: Many women say her man's help with domestic duties is a direct line to her clitoris. As a man, you may not understand it, but I suggest you believe it. Largely, this goes back to women needing to feel rested (which you can help her with by assisting with household chores). Most women view housework as essential, and child duties equally important. Your help with both of these things communications one thing: "If it's important to you, it's important to me. You are vital to our home, and I want to show appreciation and gratitude." Understand, it's not the actual job that is important, but the message that comes with your willingness to step up and do the job. Your sensitiveness and thankfulness for the roles she provides in the home (and vice versa) are paramount.

Email: Christian provided Ana with a new laptop and a blackberry JUST for emailing throughout the day. This isn't entirely necessary, of course, but this action set the stage for Ana to know that Christian wanted to be in contact with her regularly. And PING, when she hears her email or phone ding, she gets excited with anticipation. Aroused, even.

What's so hot and steamy about the email, especially if there are no overt sexual words in them? First, that they merely exist is a good start. The fact that Christian or Ana email each other to say, "Hey, baby, I'm thinking of you" shows interest in each other. But remember, it is up to BOTH of you to keep the ball in play. What I mean is, when your partner sends an email or text, you then have to ramp up your words and interject a little play into the action. What's your move?

A friend decided to send a picture of her modeling her sexy, new panties. When her partner received the text, he merely responded, "That's nice."

Uhm, "That's nice?" What that was, was taking a chance and being incredibly vulnerable, and it fell flat. What the heck does that response even mean? He didn't communicate anything to her - he definitely did not keep the ball rolling. A better response may have been, "Wow, you look hot! I can't wait to get home..."

From the subject line to the salutation, the emails are thoughtful. Here's an example of Christian sending Ana an email:

From: Christian Grey

Subject: You

To: Anastasia Steele

Dear Miss Steel,

You are quite simply exquisite. The most beautiful, intelligent, witty, and brave woman I have ever met.

Christian Grey,

CEO, Grey Enterprise Holdings Inc.

And Anastasia's email back to Christian is equally flirty:

From: Anastasia Steele

Subject: Flattery

To: Christian Grey

Dear Mr. Grey,

Flattery will get you nowhere, but since you've been everywhere the point is moot.

Ana

And so the exchange goes…

In another email exchange, Ana's subject is "Assault and Battery: The After-Effects" – this was after a rather playful evening of sex for both of them, so her subject was a joke. But it got his attention, of course. She addresses him as "Mr. Grey" and he addresses her as "Miss Steele" for effect, really. It was just a way to be playful with each other. During the same "Assault and Battery" email, Ana responds saying, "Aren't you in a meeting??" and Christian responds right back and saying, "I am in a meeting discussing the futures market, if you're really interested." And the answer is, no, she isn't interested in the meeting in the slightest, but she IS interested in the fact that he is thinking of her while in a work meeting (or at least he leads her to believe this is so). This sends the message he would rather be talking with Ana than discussing the futures market – whatever that is! Ana knows she is on his mind. She feels important. This is foreplay!

The emails are daily, multiple times a day when possible, and they range in topic:

Ana: *"My interviews went well, thought you might be interested. How was your day?"*

Christian: *"Everything you do interests me. You are the most fascinating woman I know. My morning was beyond all expectations (morning sex!). My afternoon was dull by comparison."*

Christian compliments Ana in the email exchange above – this is foreplay!

Ana: *"The morning was exemplary for me, too in spite of you weirding out on me after the impeccable desk sex. Don't think I didn't notice. I'd like to ask you about something without you weirding out on me."*

Christian: *"'Weirding' is not a verb and should not be used by anyone who wants to go into publishing. Impeccable? Compared to what, pray tell? And what do you need to ask about? I'm intrigued."*

Ana: *"Language evolves and moves on. It is an organic thing. It is not stuck in a ivory tower, hung with expensive works of art overlooking most of Seattle. Impeccable -- compared to the other times we have...what's your word...oh yes...fucked. Actually the fucking has been pretty impeccable period in my humble opinion, but then -- as you know I have very limited experience."*

Being playful is foreplay! Christian and Ana are equally playful to each other.

Ana: *"Pleasant dreams, Mr. Grey... thinking of you."*

Christian: *"Enjoy your dinner, and I miss you, especially your behind and your smart mouth. My afternoon will be dull, brightened only by thoughts of you and your eye rolling."*

Thinking of him ... foreplay! Making him a priority is also foreplay.

Christian signs that email, *"CEO & Eye Roller,"* and in Ana's reply, where she says *"You are very distracting, even when you are on the other side of the continent"* she signs, *"Your Ana."*

Taking the time to connect with your partner by expressing appreciation, love, affection, nice thoughts, and playfulness is absolutely, definitely, beyond a shadow of a doubt, foreplay. Foreplay happens now, and throughout the day.

In yet another exchange, Ana says, *"I have to go get ready"* and Christian responds, *"Can I zip up your dress?"* Ana responds, *"I would rather you unzipped it."* Of course, Christian responds, *"SO WOULD I."* The next response has the subject *"Panting"* and the message *"Slowly..."* to which Christian responds as his subject, *"Groaning"* and the message *"Wish I were there."*

The email exchanges are innocent, suggestive, flirty, sweet, loving, gentle, and rough. More than anything, they simply exist which is something we probably don't do much of in our own relationships. We don't touch base with our partners throughout the day, but if we don't, then we're not putting ourselves in the forefront of our partner's mind – a big component of foreplay. If we aren't engaging in foreplay, sex will be plain ole' vanilla (which isn't altogether bad, but it does get boring, no?) or sex won't happen at all!

Admittedly, it's not easy having these types of exchanges when you've been together for years. The flirtation between Ana and Christian occurs in the beginning of their courtship; however, as they progress through their relationship, into marriage and then with kids, they find ways to spice things up, too. The playroom Christian used to take his submissives to becomes a playroom for him and his wife. They don't mind exploring new ideas and keeping sex fresh and exciting through the use of verbalizing, body language, and of course, toys. Texts and emails are so easy, too. While they aren't an element you may be used to, I suggest giving it a try no matter what phase of your relationship you're in. In the end, we all want to know someone pines after us and finds us attractive. Let's face it; if we aren't getting the words of affirmation and acts of love from our partners, it makes it much easier to seek them out elsewhere, usually in ways that are not a healthy part of a committed partnership.

Emailing is a very simple way to let your partner know you have them on your mind. Your partner wants... no, needs to know they're in your thoughts. Keep her interested in you! She'll be thinking of your smooth, freshly shaved skin, your smell, your crisply ironed clothes, your graciousness, your "come hither" stare during your walk toward her, and the way your hands move to caress her when you finally see her again. When you DO touch her, she'll be MORE than ready to respond. (Not sure what a "come hither" stare is? It's the look that says, "I can't wait to touch you, and feel you next to me." It is a look that says, "Whoa, you're hot!" Practice it, you won't be sorry!)

Text: Be playful, inquisitive, or appreciative - it doesn't take long to let your partner know you're on their mind when you send a quick text. Even saying a simple, "Hi" speaks volumes. And, if you really want to kick things up a notch, use your words to turn her on. For example: "I just read a hot scene from Fifty Shades..." (That gets him thinking!) or "My clitoris is waiting for you..."

Show appreciation: For her smile, for his integrity, for the meal he made last night - appreciation can be found in even small acts. Christian tells Ana, "Do you have any idea what you do to me?" Uhm, well just that statement alone gives me some clue! That, coupled with his attentiveness to her body, her clothes, her smile, her job... this is important! "Your skin is flawless..." is showing appreciation. It's flirting. Flirting is foreplay!

Foreplay is essentially answering the question, "What can I do to make him feel important, loved, cherished, and adored right now?" Of course, you won't be thinking of her every minute of the day, but when you do think of her, let her know. If you aren't making a pointed effort to convey that you appreciate or cherish him, you aren't engaging in foreplay. And if you aren't engaging in foreplay, you probably won't have good sex, IF you have sex at all.

What to do now:

Tips for Men:

- Take heed if she tells you assisting with domestic jobs are important to her. Perhaps commit to just 10 minutes per day, using the time to assist in some way (you can get a lot done in 10 minutes!)
- Let your partner know what helps you with foreplay (just as domestic duties may help her).

Tips for Women:

- Some men like love notes and surprise bouquets of flowers, too. Don't be afraid to ask your partner what they like to stay turned on during the day.
- Don't be afraid to try something out of the ordinary, like texting a photo of yourself modeling your new undergarments.

- When your partner is suggestive in email, text or otherwise, be suggestive back. Be sure to respond to his advances, or the advances very well could stop!

Tips for Couples:

- Find out from your partner what she or he thinks is playful, and if playfulness is foreplay. Ask your partner how you can "come on to them" during the day, then do as they suggest! (If they don't have a suggestion right off, go out on a limb and try something new.)
- Send a playful email to your partner.
- Send an appreciative text, such as: "Thanks for such a yummy dinner last night! I love when you make that dish."
- Email or text something suggestive, such as: "I miss you..." or "I'm wearing my weighted balls right now (remember the balls from the book?)" or "I'd like to lick you all over."
- Compliment your partner, such as: "You look great in that blue sweater" or "You never cease to amaze me!" or "Wow, you smell great!"

5. Use Your Non-Verbal Body Language

Our bodies say so much! 70% of our communication is non-verbal. The emails and texts are considered verbal, even though they aren't face-to-face, and they reveal so much that is going on in your mind while you aren't within eyesight of your partner. But when you ARE together, how you act is incredibly important. Be aware of how you're perceived. What energy are you giving off? Are you a man (or woman) in control? Do you exude self-confidence? Are you respectful? Are you genuine, in love, caring, intrigued, and interested? Most importantly, what do you think your body is communicating at any given moment? Remember, foreplay is happening right now. If your husband or wife is glancing your way, what message are you sending?

We all want to be swept off our feet. We want our spouses to communicate they love us fully and unconditionally, but what exactly does that mean?

Small clues show your love, especially if the clues come from your body. Numerous times throughout the books, Christian is caught staring at Ana, gazing at her, or with his mouth gaped open as if he was undressing her with his eyes. She could tell by his stare that he couldn't get enough of her.

During sexual moments, it was clear on both sides how the other was feeling, and not just because one of them said, "That feels so good (which they did say!)" but also because of their facial expressions and the way they positioned their body.

On more occasions than I can count, Christian touches Ana in the minutes before intercourse in a way that expressed his need for her. He longed to have her aroused, because having her aroused made him aroused in turn! He cupped her breasts, pulled her nipples, sucked her nipples, kissed her naval, bit her bottom, caressed her bottom, ran small kisses over her entire body, touched her inner thighs, nibbled on her neck, softly kissed her neck, and nibbled on her earlobes. When Christian Grey was near Ana Steele, he couldn't keep his hands and lips off of her! Every action he made told her she was attractive to him, and he wanted her. Her gentle touch aroused him. Ana got the message when he pressed his erection into her and he breathed ragged and heavy on her neck and in her hair. At other times, he closed his eyes and tossed his head back in ecstasy, moaning, groaning, and sighing deep sounds of need. And, he did it constantly. His non-verbal cues told Ana she was desperately wanted and needed, and when he gave her those cues, she felt beautiful, sexy, and loved.

Mr. Grey ran his hands down Miss Steele's cheeks, softly kissed her lips, gripped her hair to pull her into him, caressed her bottom, ran his index finger along her lips, rubbed her nose, and leaned forehead-to-forehead to gaze into her eyes.

Many actions Christian and Ana did were an act of love. After all, this is an erotic love story! More importantly, they engaged in constant acts of foreplay. A small touch, slight glance, and a soft whisper say so much. Eye contact and letting your partner know you love the sight of them, communicates desire.

Here's an example of a hot exchange:

He plants a soft kiss under my earlobe while his fingers tighten in my hair. Pulling my head back, he exposes my throat to his lips. His teeth skim my chin, and he kisses my throat.

"I want you," he breathes.

I moan and reach up and grasp his arms.

The non-verbal communication AND his words are so descriptive.

He clasps his hands on either side of my head and kisses me. Deeply. Possessing my mouth. Angling my head … controlling me. I moan against his lips. … He groans shifting me so I'm astride him, kneeling over him, his erection beneath me … his eyes [are] hooded and lustful. "I'm going to have you now," he whispers.

Uhm, okay. You have me now. That "take charge" confidence is enticing! Most women want a commanding, passionate man, and some men want their woman to also be dominant and eager at times. The take-charge actions we initiate communicate, simply, "I want you, I can't stand not being with you, and I'm going to have you now, you are mine…"

Your body language broadcasts what you're thinking and feeling more than your actual words. Be aware of what you're saying. Even while watching TV, while reading your book, while sitting across from each other in a booth at a restaurant, while pouring yourself a glass of wine, while mowing the lawn, while cleaning out flower beds, while getting dressed, while taking a shower, while sleeping… most actions are our a signals for what we're thinking and feeling. You are telling your partner something about you with every wince, every breath, every hand signal, every slouch, every snore, everything. Likewise, your partner is conveying their own messages, and it is important to pay attention. Body language is extraordinarily meaningful. (But no pressure, just be yourself! □)

Allow me to drive this point home a bit more…

When you do offensive, boorish things around your partner, it very well could be a huge turn off. If she doesn't want you plucking your nose hairs in her presence, don't. If she'd rather you close the door while you do your bathroom business, do. Don't flatulate in front of him – it's gross, it's a turnoff, and he won't want to have sex with the girl who just stank up the place (unless he's into that sort of thing, and who am I to judge?). Don't belch in front of her either. Does she want her mouth on yours after what just came out of it? And for God's sake, brush your teeth after you eat. Do you think he wants to smell the garlic on your breath, or taste it in his mouth? No, he does not.

Wear clean clothes that smell good, and make sure they fit like they're supposed to. She doesn't want to see your grubby, grimy, stained clothing – it's a huge turnoff. Communicate you care about your appearance, and she'll communicate she cares about your appearance, too! If you don't respect your own body language and attire, she isn't going to respect you, either.

Throughout the book, Christian wore jeans and a clean white shirt. That was all Ana needed to be turned on! His pants hung "just so" off his hips, and he always smelled like "body soap and Christian." Ana said she wanted to bury herself in his chest and inhale him...often. The chemistry was electrifying.

When you find him hot, tell him, even with your gaze. If he says something to you, listen. When he tells you about his day, let him know there's no one on planet earth you'd rather be hearing about in this moment. When he vents his frustration, use your ears to listen, and close your mouth.

When you're aroused, tell her. Show her. Let her touch you. Touch her while she's touching you.

Communicate with your body. Every action hints at a feeling and thought about something – what is your body disclosing? The important point to understand is that our non-verbal language, our body language, is communicating whether we are speaking or not. Use your words, but realize your body is also speaking on your behalf as well.

What to do now:

Tips for Men:

- Do you like to know when your woman is aroused? If so, tell her you'd like a sign that communicates her desire. It's often hard to tell with women, so don't be afraid to ask her for more expressiveness.
- Gaze at her...longingly. I know, I know...this isn't something you think to do all the time. But think about it - sitting across the booth at a favorite restaurant, or while she's washing dishes, it would be such a perk to see you ogle at her. Try kissing her neck while she washes dishes, too...or play footsies!

Tips for Women:

- Do you like to know when your man is aroused? Let him know, and he can tell you with his body.
- Nuzzle him, kiss his chest, and tell him you find him attractive and hot when you do.

Tips for Couples:

- Reexamine your clothing choices. Make sure they fit correctly, aren't stained, and smell good.
- Don't save shaving and showers just for the office. There's important work to be done at home, too! Make sure you keep yourself clean and smelling fresh in all your body parts.
- Your husband doesn't want to feel your leg stubble, or see your unplucked chin hairs. Your wife doesn't want to see your unplucked brow hair, either! Take heed, and groom regularly.
- Pay attention to your own body – it sends messages even when you don't use your words. If your partner reads the language of your body right now, what message are they receiving?
- Brush and floss regularly.
- Use your ears and eyes to listen. Closing your mouth means you're receiving what your partner says with an open heart.
- Open a discussion about preferences. For example, if you prefer your wife in matching undergarments, tell her. Better

yet, buy some for her! If you prefer your husband to wear nothing but his briefs without holes, let him know.

- Above all, be respectful when communicating your desires with your partner. Hearing the message that you'd like something changed can be taken as criticism when not presented in a loving, caring, and positive manner.

6. Use Music to Set the Mood

Music evokes intense, powerful feelings. It has power to create a mood and change a mood. Our emotions can change because of the melodies that stream through our ears, often igniting memories we may not be aware we have. A song can bring up good memories and bad memories. They elicit emotions deep within our being, igniting feelings we can't readily touch without a musical reminder.

Christian and Ana share a love of music. Christian has eclectic tastes, and he likes to use music to create a scene he wants to play out with Ana. He uses music as a form of expression when his own words fail to convey what he longs to communicate to his beloved Ana.

Always at the ready, Christian's iPod is filled with melodic tunes he dials to in an instant, setting the mood for him and Ana, and the activity they are engaged in, whether it is taking a long drive, hang gliding, sailing, making love, or having sex.

I differentiate between sex and making love because there is a distinct difference. I often remind couples of this distinction in our therapy and coaching sessions. This is the main problem in this story, after all. Ana wants Christian to make love to her, but Christian isn't comfortable with that closeness - with the raw emotion and sensuality that comes with making love. He isn't comfortable with the vulnerability. He isn't comfortable being touched, hence his need to dominate and control. By being in control, he knows when and where he will be touched. He creates the rules, and you play by his rules, or you don't play. Except that, he is interested in a relationship with Ana - he wants something more - and he slowly drifts from his comfort zone to have that "more." (I'll go more in depth about the "more" in Part 7, coming up next!)

Sex is just the act of sex. You have an act with the end in mind - an orgasm. Usually, there is nothing more to this than the physical act of sex. Not much, if any foreplay, and certainly not the minute-by-minute foreplay I've discussed previously.

Making love (intimacy and passion) is an extension of the emotion you feel for your partner. It is an extension of your love, and when you have this kind of love, you make yourself vulnerable, expressing your passion and raw, intense emotion.

Many couples get to a point in their relationship of just having sex. Sex is done mindlessly in a "let's-get-this-over-quick" fashion. Frankly, it is this type of sex that has couples turned off of sex. At least one person in the relationship feels slighted because they don't feel the emotional connection - the intimacy and passion - that they need to have while making love. They ultimately feel used during the act, which is the main reason sex gets avoided altogether.

Through music, it becomes increasingly evident how Christian feels for Ana. He even makes her a song list in the second book, and attached to the song list is a note saying that the songs convey for him, what he is unable to provide through his own words. Christian's song list to Ana includes:

"Witchcraft" by Frank Sinatra that says:

Those fingers in my hair

That sly come hither stare

That strips my conscience bare

It's witchcraft

"Try" by Nelly Furtado whose lyrics say:

Then I see you standing there

Wanting more from me

And all I can do is try...

"Spem in Alium" by Thomas Tallis - A favorite of Christians, he played Thomas Tallis while he seduced Ana in his great room. It evokes emotion in both of them. From the late 1500s and originally in Latin, the English translation is:

I have never put my hope in any other but in you,

O God of Israel

Who can show both anger

And graciousness,

And who absolves all the sins of suffering man

Lord God,

Creator of Heaven and Earth

Be mindful of our lowliness

Bach Marcello - An instrumental piece, reminiscent of when Christian plays his sad, melodic tunes when he can't sleep in the early morning hours. This song makes Ana's heart ache for him. She knows he is a wounded, sad soul, despite his controlling exterior.

"Lightning Strike" by Snow Patrol - Ana's favorite band. Christian including this one shows he is tuned in to her - he knows what she likes. This song is over 26 minutes long:

What if this storm ends?

And I don't see you

As you are now

Ever again

The perfect halo

Of gold hair and lightning

Sets you off against

The planet's last dance

And...

And in the middle of the flood I felt my worth

When you held onto me like I was your little life raft

Please know that you were mine as well

Drops of water hit the ground like God's own tears

And spread out into shapes like

Salad bowls and basins and buckets for bailing out the flood

"Principles of Lust" by Enigma:

The principles of lust... Are easy to understand

Do what you feel... Feel until the end

The principles of lust... Are burnt in your mind

Do what you want... Do it until you find Love...

"Possession" - It's unclear in the story who this song is by, but the title alone says something about Christian's thinking.

"The Scientist" by Coldplay which says:

Nobody said it was easy

It’s such a shame for us to part

Nobody said it was easy

No one ever said it would be this hard

Other music is featured throughout all three books. The carefully selected sounds emanate through the scenes in which Christian and Ana engage. They evoke strong emotion in both of them, and they seem to be carefully planned for the moments they are played.

"The Flower Duet" by Léo Delibes’ opera Lakmé is a famous duet first performed in Paris in 1883. Christian’s iPod streams “the sweetest, most magical music of two women singing” in his car the day after he rescues Ana from a friend who is inappropriately coming on to her at a bar. She spends the night in Christian’s hotel room, but they don’t engage in sex, only a passionate kiss in the elevator. The song, originally written in French but translated to English, is a glimpse into the eclectic world that is Christian Grey.

In the same car ride, the attraction growing between them, Christian tunes his iPod to Kings of Leon's "Sex on Fire.” Ana thinks, “How appropriate.” And it is. The sexual energy and tension build for both Christian and Ana. It’s a popular song:

You, your sex is on fire

Consumed with what's to transpire

Hot as fever, rattling bones

I could just taste it, taste it

If its not forever, if it’s just tonight

Damien Rice drones a melodic, sensual tune as he belts out words in "The Blowers Daughter":

I can't take my eyes off you

I can't take my eyes off you

I can't take my eyes off you

Again and again deliberate choices of music are used to set the backdrop to Christian and Ana's flirtatious courtship and ensuing relationship. Ana takes note of the song selections, feeling Christian's emotional depth, and his conveyance of messages he can't readily call up on his own.

In the playroom, while Ana's wrists and ankles are tethered to the bed, a blindfold on so she can't see what Christian is going to do, he puts headphones on her to set a mood. Once, he plays a soft instrumental. Afterward he says, "I've always wanted to fuck to that."

Yet another time in the play room, Christian pipes in "Sex Slave" by Deadmau5, a techno beat that gives a different feel. The lyrics say:

Strip me down and go to town

Lick me over upside down

Pound and pound and pound and pound

Baby make me make that sound

In the first song, there is a more sensual, passionate feel. In the second song, there is a hard, raw, erotic, "I'm going to fuck you now" feel. There's a pleasurable result at the end of each, obviously. The music sets the mood. One thing is for sure, their sex is rarely plain ole' vanilla!

In book three, Christian sits at the piano in his parent's house playing while everyone else is mingling in another room. Unaware he's being watched, Christian begins to play Roberta Flack's "The First Time Ever I Saw Your Face." He played it another time in book two after Ana requested rather playful sex in the playroom. Christian says after their play time, "This is what I want to do…" then he proceeds to make love to Ana, slowly, to this tune:

The first time ever I saw your face

I thought the sun rose in your eyes

And the moon and stars were the gifts you gave

To the dark and empty skies, my love

The first time ever I kissed your mouth

And felt your heart close to mine

Like the trembling heart of a captive bird

That was there at my command, my love

And the first time, ever I lay with you

I felt your heart so close to mine

And I knew our joy would fill the earth

And last till the end of time my love

It would last till the end of time.

This song seems to be a sort of anthem for both of them.

The songs Christian played for Ana say so much. In real life, we won't always have music and sex won't always be "kinky fuckery." But in a relationship that needs a pick-me-up - in a sex life that needs to be rejuvenated - music can stimulate our emotional and sexual senses. Being thoughtful about your choice of music is important. What does the song say that you can't say to your partner? What emotions get riled up by this song? What emotions do you want to elicit from your partner?

Christian says in Fifty Shades Darker, "Anticipation is the key to seduction." True! Use music as part of the seduction. Remember, foreplay is happening now. Allow music to help set your sensual, sexual, loving, passionate mood

What to do now:

Tips for Couples:

- Buy an iPod or some other musical device to which you can stream music. Then, create a playlist boasting favorite tunes of both you and your partner. Play music anytime you want to create a mood - while cooking dinner, mowing the lawn, working out, taking a bath, cleaning house, and having sex, just to name a few.
- Create a song list for your partner. Make sure these are songs that you know they will love, and that reminds you of them.
- Download a song that says what you want to say, but can't, then email it to your partner. Or, play the song for them, and dance together.

- If you play an instrument, play it for your partner! Nothing is sexier than seeing your emotion come through the strings on your guitar or the keys on your piano.

7. Trust, Love and Respect Each Other

In Fifty Shades of Grey, Christian proposed a BDSM relationship to Ana. She is introduced to a world she has never even heard of, let alone experienced. Ana is met with a huge dilemma. On the one hand, she feels a magnetism to Christian she has never felt. At 21 years of age, she hasn't had a long term relationship, and she hasn't yet had sex. She considers herself strong-willed – someone who is saving herself for the right man. On the other hand, she is dismayed by Christian's alternative lifestyle, if not downright frightened.

At the same time, Christian is mesmerized by Ana. As the Frank Sinatra song says, "It's witchcraft." Christian was also experiencing a gravitational pull toward Ana, and in a way he had never experienced. Ana wasn't interested in signing contracts and following Christian's rules. She wanted a "real" relationship, not one in which she is dominated by someone interested in nothing but sex.

Christian tells Ana he has never had a "real" relationship, that BDSM is the only kind of relationship of which he is interested. Ana said she has never had a long term relationship either, so she doesn't necessarily know the rules of the relationship game, but she feels quite sure the "rules" don't look like the dominant/submissive one he is proposing. Christian asks Ana to just try a relationship on his terms, and asks Ana to trust him. She isn't sure she can trust someone who so eagerly wants to hurt her for his pleasure, and likewise, asks him to just try for a "normal" courtship. She tells Christian she wants more in a relationship - more love, more trust, more respect, and more love-making, which she differentiates from just having sex (as discussed in the previous section). Christian says matter-of-factly, "I don't make love. I fuck. Hard."

Christian's dominance is a turn on for Ana. He is straightforward, but respectful. Ana feels a real chemistry with Christian, despite his need for power. Admittedly, she is shocked that she even contemplates the possibility of using kinky toys, being tied up, or being spanked. However, although Ana is intrigued by Christian's lifestyle, she knows she has no desire to be hurt physically. In fact, she is fearful of pain. She has hard limits that will undoubtedly keep her from fully entering into the type of relationship he proposes. Still, Christian doesn't want to let Ana go.

Despite the fact that Christian is fearful of the "more" Ana craves from him, he continues to pursue her. Likewise, whereas Ana cannot see herself in a BDSM relationship, and she wants something more than Christian says he can offer, she continues to stay on Christian's radar. These two have a chemistry with each other that is "bewitching." Bewitching is the term Christian uses to describe his pull toward Ana.

By the end if Fifty Shades of Grey, Ana has tried some of Christian's dominant world of which she surprisingly finds she enjoys. In one instance, Christian puts Ana over his knee and spanks her. She consents to the spanking, says she wants to try it, and in fact, admits that she feels more pleasure than pain from the experience. Despite knowing Christian for such a short amount of time, she trusts him not to hurt her. She knows she can say no anytime. Still, Ana longs for a different kind of a relationship, and when Christian shows his dominance one evening in a way that is painful for Ana, she leaves him. She makes a decision to disengage from him, denying his relationship proposal.

In Fifty Shades Darker, Ana and Christian's relationship shifts dramatically. When Ana leaves Christian and denies his proposal, he feels like he has lost a piece of his soul. He is surprised by his own despair, and the love he feels for Ana. Her rejection is excruciating – a feeling he has never experienced in all his BDSM affairs. That pain awakens something familiar in him. He has felt that pain before...

Christian begins to want Ana's "more." More than anything, he simply wants Ana. And he tells her, in no uncertain terms, "I want you however I can have you." If that means a relationship that is outside of his dominant/submissive bounds, so be it. In fact, Christian begins to shift from a world of needing to have control, to a world of understanding his need for the control.

As their relationship grows through Fifty Shades Darker and into Fifty Shades Freed, Christian and Ana begin to trust each other implicitly. It is only because of this trust that Ana knows Christian will never hurt her. Likewise, Christian begins to desire a "real" relationship with Ana – one in which he would never hurt her, even a little. In fact, the thought pains him. He won't even go into the play room with Ana – his "red room of pain" as Ana called it, where he took all of his submissives to have his way with them. Christian says he doesn't need that lifestyle any longer. He thinks about the BDSM, but he doesn't feel drawn to it. He doesn't feel like he has to have that kind of dominant/submissive relationship with Ana. On the contrary, Christian now desperately wants "more" from Ana, and he will do anything to please her. He will do anything to win her trust and love, and show her he will never hurt her, "even if she begs," he tells her.

Within their new spark for each other – their renewed trusting relationship – is the desire to become better, and experience life differently, especially for Christian. Christian has only engaged in dominant/submissive relationships where the submissives were forbidden from touching him, looking at him, or even saying his first name. They called him "Sir."

As time moves on, Ana gets glimpses of Christian's inner world - a world he hasn't revealed to anyone. He has a lot of emotional pain hidden behind his facade of power and control. Christian has never confided in anyone the reasons for his need to dominate women the way he does. He is a successful business man, and his control and dominance shows up there, too. He is commanding, and it is a turn on for Ana, but she recognizes his abuse of power. He begins to recognize his abuse of power too, as they begin opening up to each other about his past life.

Christian doesn't want Ana to touch him on his stomach, chest, or back. Ana realizes this is a reason he wants to tie her up (although, as their relationship evolves, they continue to restrain each other in their sexual acts, but it's not for control reasons, it is merely adult play. It is "kinky fuckery" – a term Ana uses to describe their sexual playfulness.). The reasons Christian doesn't want to be touched, and the reason for his overwhelming need for control, is because of the abuse he endured at the hands of his biological mother - a "crack whore" - until the age of 4. He watched his mother die, and it took four days for authorities to find him. He spent a few months in foster care until he was adopted by the Grey family. Then, at the age of 15 a family friend began sexually and physically abusing Christian. He was a "submissive" to an older, powerful woman until the age of 21. After that relationship, he began his own world of being a dominant, never entering into "real" relationships, but only BDSM ones. He lost his childhood to a crack whore and he lost his adolescence to a dominant, sexually abusive woman. Now, at 26 years of age, he meets Ana, feeling something he never thought he would feel. Christian created a world of walls - a world where he was intent on keeping people out so he could not be hurt by them. But when Ana says the only way she will have a relationship with him is if it's "normal" and not a dominant/submissive one, Christian has to learn to break down his walls. He begins to let Ana in.

In book two, Fifty Shades Darker, Ana has several epiphanies about her beloved Christian:

- "He likes me to be tethered. I can't touch him this way. ... That's why he likes his rules." She now recognizes why he wants to tie her up. He can't bear to be touched by anyone, including Ana, because of his sexual abuse history.
- Christian says to her, "I'm nothing, Anastasia. I'm a husk of a man. I don't have a heart." Christian feels as if he isn't worthy of being loved; that in fact, no one loves him. He views himself as a sick, twisted man.
- Ana reflects, "I am overwhelmed by his trust in me - overwhelmed by his fear, by the damage done to this beautiful, fallen, flawed man." Ana begins to see Christian's trust in her, and she knows she is the only one he has ever trusted. She knows he is changing because of the love and trust he feels for her.

Through their honest communication, both verbal and nonverbal, they begin to explore each other's inner lives. Christian trusts Ana and begins to open up to her about his childhood, divulging more and more details of the horrendous abuse he endured as a child. Ana loves Christian unconditionally, and this allows for his raw, intense inner exploration and ultimate change.

In truth, all of us want to have this unconditional love. We want to know that despite our flaws, we are loveable. Each of us has a primal need for affection, respect, truth and honesty, which are demonstrations of being unconditionally loved. These needs began as a baby, fresh out of the womb. Truly, none of us are born with "issues." We weren't manipulative, needing power and control, or acting out with substances to get our needs met as babies and toddlers, obviously. But, when our needs aren't met, through time, we develop coping skills to feel loved and worthy in adulthood.

Having a loving, nurturing relationship at the onset of our lives with our caregivers sets us up for success in many ways – career, intimate relationships, friendships, etc. How we learn to give and receive love with our caregivers then carries over into our own intimate relationships. We find our life partner based on these needs and the coping skills we learned during our early childhood. When we find someone who we connect with on this deep, fundamental, core level, we can't think of being with anyone but this person. To lose this person would be like cutting off a limb. It would mean losing our "safe place." We will go to great lengths for this person, to keep them. We need them physically, emotionally, cognitively, and spiritually.

In real life, when someone does not receive or know unconditional love - when they don't have the trusting person they know loves them no matter what - life is filled with many hardships. Physically, spiritually, emotionally or cognitively, a person who does not have that safe, secure place in which to thrive, endures a life of loneliness, despair, and sadness. There is a broken spirit - a lost soul - within a person who hasn't felt and doesn't feel the security of a trusting, loving human being. There is no safe place to grow.

A lost soul acts erratically, trying desperately to find something externally to fill their internal void. Drug abuse, adultery, sex addiction, over eating, insomnia, and chronic fatigue are just a handful of examples of ways we use to cure that brokenness we feel. We attempt to do wonderful, powerful things to help us feel loved, respected, and trusted, but that love, respect, and trust for others and ourselves is often superficial and short-lived. One doesn't experience true joy or a lifetime of happiness when their soul is secretly crushed.

Christian used his BDSM lifestyle to fill the void in his soul. He used his power and control to help him feel the respect and trust he craved. He longed to feel loved, but he found that superficial love in all the wrong ways since he had a huge emotional barrier up to protect himself.

This message – the message of trust because of unconditional love - is the real story of Fifty Shades of Grey. It is only because of the trust these two have that they share their lives with each other in this new and complicated way. Ana explores "kinky fuckery" and Christian explores "making love." Where Christian had an intense need for control because of his childhood fears that were never resolved, he created a BDSM lifestyle. It wasn't until he started releasing his fear and began coming to terms with his childhood traumas that his need for control began to cease. AND, he could only step out of that fear because of his new, trusting relationship with the one who shows her unconditional love for him, Ana. Christian trusts Ana. Ana trusts Christian.

Some never find this kind of love. Some people skip from relationship to relationship, unsure why they never stick - why they fight, argue, and end up being left ... or leaving. It's painful for a relationship to end, but the kind of relationships that are entered into with severe problems - problems brought from childhood - are ones that are in danger of never being healthy. These relationships suffer without intervention. People who enter into relationships as lost souls, often remain lost souls. People who enter into relationships as lost souls, often marry lost souls because lose souls gravitate to each other. Misery loves company.

Christian's intervention is Ana. She was unexpected...

"As ever, Miss Steele, you are unexpected."

Ana suspects his controlling tendencies are because of his childhood:

"He thinks he doesn't deserve to be loved. Why does he feel that way? Does it have to do with his upbringing? His birth mom, the crack whore?"

Christian, unraveling at the seams with his new, unexpected love, confirms what Ana is beginning to learn about Christian: "You could have a nice brunette submissive. One who would ask 'How high?' every time you asked her to jump, provided she had permission to speak. So why me, Christian, I just don't get it?" Christian replies, "You make me look at the world differently, Anastasia. You give me ... hope. ... There's something about you Anastasia, that calls to me on some deep level I don't understand."

Ana reflects, "He says nothing, just gazes at me. All I see is his desire, his adoration even. And something else, the depth of his need - the depth of his love for me."

This is all the mushy stuff of a relationship that some have and some don't. You may not be mushy in your own relationship, but the point is this: Trust in your partner has to be established above all else before any semblance of a relationship can grow to the depths it can potentially blossom, especially sexually. This essential trust is unconditional, healthy love. BDSM can be unhealthy when practiced as a lost soul. It isn't love at all when it's used the way Christian Grey used it for power and control. But bondage can be used in a healthy relationship. This is what Ana calls “kinky fuckery" – it is play time between two people that love each other.

There is so much focus on the sex in this relationship. Admittedly, the sex is good! It's really good. But why is it so good? Why are women so taken with Christian Grey? After all, there are hundreds of erotica books to read, porn to watch, and magazines to give you ideas to spice up your own sex life.

The answer is way simple: Women are smitten with Christian because he loves, adores...no, he cherishes Anastasia, and he shows her again and again and again. These two love each other so fully and unconditionally, they have freedom in their sex. They don't feel inhibited, untrusting, or shy. Their sex is an extension of their love – isn't this what each of us want in our bedrooms when we get right down to it? Sure, there are times we want to just fuck. Hard. But even then, we are able to have that adult play time, fucking hard, when we are in a loving, trusting, healthy relationship.

In my conversations with friends who are so taken with this book and with Christian Grey, it is the love affair that that gets talked about again and again. Women want to be cherished. They want to feel the unconditional love Christian shows for Ana. The truth is though; we all want to feel cherished! Men aren't reading this book because it isn't marketed to men (and honestly, with reviews that tout a billionaire who abuses and disrespects women through sex, why would they??). But the bottom line story of this book is universal for men and women. The love story is one we all want!

Here's what's key: Christian and Ana are tuned in to each other. Christian knows what Ana wants because he WANTS to know, first and foremost. And, his actions follow through. He wants to keep this woman, his healer in many ways. He wants to love her in all the ways she needs to be loved. We hear Ana repeatedly tell him she doesn't need his money, and he is surprised by this. The truth is, she doesn't feel loved through his gifts. She feels loved in the way he touches her, kisses her, talks to her, and regards her. She trusts him to hear her. He trusts her to be tuned in. They trust each other at a deep, profound and intimate level, and because they trust each other so fully - trust that they won't be hurt by being who they are - they are free to love fully. Loving freely, they are uninhibited with each other, free to explore the boundaries of their relationship, and step out over the boundaries together.

What to do now:

If you can't freely open up to your partner, and it is negatively impacting your relationship, I suggest you seek professional help. Of all the steps in this guide, this is the most important one. You won't be able to send a loving text, engage in fantasies, or talk about how to ramp up your foreplay without absolute trust in your partner.

Tips for Couples:

- Show trust in your partner by engaging in difficult conversations, like ones suggested in this guide. You can also show trust by talking about your own inner world – what you feel, what your think, your opinions, etc.

- Open a dialogue about your partner's childhood. Find out what they learned from their caregivers and the relationships they witnessed growing up.

- When your partner opens up about a difficult issue, don't be afraid of what they say. Listen with your ears and eyes, and ask your partner how you can comfort them. Also, don't bring this issue up at an inappropriate time. For example, it's not okay to say during the middle of an argument, "You're angry at me now because your father was as angry at you as a child!" There is a time and place for that statement, but the middle of an argument, when it feels like you are "throwing this in their face" is the wrong time.

- Show your partner unconditional positive regard, regardless of what they say or do. If change needs to happen in a specific area of your partner's life, they probably already know it. Accepting them "as is" is the best way to show your love. When there is something you simply cannot tolerate, and view as a slight to you personally, take personal inventory to find out if this really is a slight toward you, or if it's really their issue. If it is their issue, let them keep it, and you simply love them through it.

- Pick up a copy of Gary Chapman's "The Five Love Languages" and figure out how your partner best receives love. If you enjoy touching your partner as an expression of your love, but your partner enjoys time alone, you could be missing the mark.

- Speak your love to your partner. For example, "My heart fills with joy when you walk into a room." And, "You were on my mind all day today. Those were good thoughts…"

- Seek to be gracious when pointing out your partner's flaws. Be respectful and courteous, even when there is a negative message to be delivered.
- Be willing to accept feedback and correction from your partner. If it is a healthy relationship, they often know you better than anyone, and can offer you some sound, loving advice that no one else may be willing to share so openly with you.
- Pick up a copy of Don Miguel Ruiz's "The Four Agreements: A Practical Guide to Personal Freedom (A Toltec Wisdom Book)." Take heed in the four agreements, which are:
    1. Be impeccable with your word.
    2. Don't take anything personally.
    3. Don't make assumptions.
    4. Always do your best.

Look, I know this guide is largely with a female slant. In my experience as a therapist, however, both men and women want all the things mentioned in this guide. Above all, men want to be respected and women want to be cherished. By demonstrating respect for your man, you show love. By demonstrating your adoration for your woman, you show love.

Men might be reading this book, but I don't know. If they are, they aren't admitting it. Women, however, are reading it and loving it. Women are obsessed. And yes, we get that this is a book of fiction. We get that this relationship isn't real. Women get that our obsessions are...strange. We're mystified by the attraction! That's the main reason I opened up a discussion with friends about Fifty Shades, sought to understand, and wrote this guide. Women can't get enough of Christian Grey, Ana Steele, and this incredible love story, steeped in unconditional love and healing. Now, hopefully you know why.

In summary, there are several key areas that will spice up your relationship now:

1. Consider the unspoken rules of your relationship. That is, take heed in how you present yourself to your partner. Are you well-groomed with nice, clean clothes? Are you taking care of your physical appearance?

2. Know how your partner likes to be touched. Do you know how your partner pleasures herself or himself? Do you know what it takes for your partner to truly enjoy sex and have an orgasm? Have you considered specific changes you may need to make to help please your partner between the sheets?
3. Explore each other's fantasies. Do you know your partner's fantasies? What are their hard and soft limits? When is the last time you explored each other's bodies and kicked up the action in the bedroom a few notches? Are you open to engaging in kinky fuckery? Is your partner?
4. Engage in foreplay, now! Are you aware how you present yourself to your partner, even when you aren't talking? Have you considered specific ways you can show interest in your partner, such as helping with domestic chores, sending suggestive emails and texts, and showing your appreciation?
5. Watch your body language. What does your body language say to your partner? Do you look at her suggestively? Is your tone harsh? Is there a gruff or sensual way about you? Ultimately, are you sending the message you want to send to your love?
6. Use music to set a mood or send a message. If you play an instrument, have you played for your partner? Have you considered sharing a song with your partner that says what you cannot say? Have you used music to set the mood in the bedroom?
7. Reexamine your trust, respect and love for your partner. Do you trust each other? What can you do to convey your unconditional love, creating a safe space for him or her? Have you created an environment that your partner can feel trusting of you, ready and willing to explore out of their comfort zone?

The suggestions in this guide may seem like a no-brainer. You may decide they're not worth the effort. Nevertheless, this is what women are talking about, and if you're interested in spicing up your relationship in the bedroom and otherwise, this is a good place to start! This guide doesn't replace great works of therapy, rooted in years of research. I'm a fan of marital therapy, especially drawing from the works of world-renowned therapists. This guide obviously does not replace, or even compare to true intervention. But for a mostly healthy relationship looking to get the ball rolling in the bedroom or to step up their communication of love to their partner, the tips in this guide will sure stimulate and rejuvenate a tired, boring relationship in a quickie (pun intended)!

Shades of Grey User's Guide Cheat Sheet

1. Respect the unspoken (or spoken) rules in your relationship by taking care of yourself physically, cognitively, emotionally and spiritually. The image we give off – the energy we bring to a room, the confidence we exude, and the cleanliness we have – those all matter.

2. Get to know your partner's body very well in order to keep sex pleasurable. The only way you're going to please your partner sexually is to ask them what they want and like, and then practice, practice, practice! Have an honest and frank conversation about what is and is not working, and don't be afraid to try new things.

3. Talk about your sexual fantasies. What you do in the bedroom is consensual, adult play. It is private, and it is up to you what you do in there. But you can't do anything except basic "let's-get-this-finished sex" if you don't talk about what else you can do beyond that. Talk about your fantasies, and then make a commitment to indulge.

4. Realize that foreplay happens every minute of the day, not just in the minutes before sex. Foreplay happens all day, every day. What you choose to do now will affect what happens in the bedroom - IF something happens. In the moments before sex, this is the time to enjoy each other and the arousal you've been creating throughout the day.

5. Become aware of your non-verbal communication – body language, gestures and actions. You are telling your partner something about you with every wince, every breath, every hand signal, every slouch, every snore, everything.

6. Use music to set the mood or to convey words you aren't able to say yourself. A song can bring up good memories and bad memories. They elicit emotion deep within our being, igniting feelings we can't readily touch without a music reminder.

7. Have an open, trusting relationship in order to grow together. We want to know that despite our flaws, we are loveable. Each of his has a primal need for affection, respect, truth and honesty, which is a demonstration of being unconditionally loved.

About Jennifer Slingerland Ryan, M.Ed., LPC

Jennifer is a Licensed Professional Counselor. As the founder of I Choose Change PLLC, she has worked in the mental health industry for close to 15 years and has been in private practice for over almost 10 years.

Her counseling technique is "cognitive behavioral therapy, sprinkled with a bit of spirituality." The principles of cognitive-behavioral therapy (CBT) and Attachment Theory are what she most adheres to in her work with both individuals and couples. She believes that early relationships create a blueprint for ALL other relationships throughout the lifespan, and our job is to change early processing and belief systems that keep you feeling stuck. Through their work together, her clients learn core principles of the change process, including:

- How early family relationships create a subconscious pattern of behavior in all other relationships throughout the lifespan (intimate, friends, co-workers, etc.)
- How thoughts, emotions, and actions are connected
- How early relationships create subconscious belief systems that drive everything we feel and do
- The role personality, intuition, and mindfulness play in the change process
- How homework and journal exercises between sessions make change happen more quickly
- How meditation, self-talk, role-playing, and role rehearsal affect the change process

In her work as a relationship counselor, she closely follows the same principles as outlined in attachment theory and cognitive behavioral theory, just as within individual therapy. Jennifer believes healthy individuals make healthy intimate partners. Often, relationship counseling starts as individual counseling so we can build a foundation for a healthy marriage.

She has been a partner to her husband for over 16 years and is Mom to 6 year old twin daughters and a 1 year old daughter – her most important job, by far! The balance between life roles (wife, mom, therapist, etc.) creates an unwavering desire to help others who are in need more harmony in their home and relationships.

For more information about Jennifer Slingerland Ryan, M.Ed., LPC-S, visit http://www.ichoosechange.com.

10020252R00039

Made in the USA
San Bernardino, CA
02 April 2014